# About the Cover

## Pictogram

*After Rothko*

In the painting, a herd of wild ponies
Runs across an imaginary plain.
The red palomino above is love.
The white horse below is grief,

For Willam and Nancy

# CRUMBS TOO

*Poems by*
*Richard Harteis*

Poets' Choice Publishing

Copyright © 2024. Poets' Choice Publishing

All rights reserved.

Cover Art : "Crumbs Too"

Cover Design : Sanket Patel

Artist : Anne Marchand

Graphic Design : Sanket Patel

Author Portait Back Cover: Painting by Rick Williams

Printed in the United States of America

Library of Congress Cataloging-in-Publication Data Pending

ISBN- 978-1-7371653-4-7

POETS' CHOICE PUBLISHING
AVERY HEIGHTS, SUITE 126
300 BRANDEGEE AVENUE
GROTON, CT 06340
POETS-CHOICE.COM
MARATHONFILM@GMAIL.COM

# INTRODUCTION

This is the introduction to the previous book, CRUMBS. It can serve as the introduction to CRUMBS TOO. The only addition I would make is to explain that these are additional poems employing the same style as the original poems. Happily, they are inspired by poets such as Rilke and William Carlos Williams, for example, who believe in the careful observation of the particulars in the life, and Eckhart Tolle whose philosophy of mindfulness also informs the work.

This volume includes the paintings by Anne Marchand, the 2023 Nancy Frankel Awardee for Art. Here is a photo of her and Nancy Frankel at a joint exhibition along with Margery Goldberg, Gallery Director of the Zenith Gallery: (You can purchase any of the paintings included here by contacting the Zenith Gallery in Washington: URL : ZenithGallery.com; art@ZenithGallery.com). It is appropriate then, and serendipitous to have these beautiful paintings accompany the "crumbs" found in this volume. As outlined in the original introduction, they are not meant to "illustrate" the poems, but enhance the sensation of floating in zero gravity as beautiful visual landmarks for the soul.

Anne Marchand was the 2023 recipient of this award, and it is extremely generous of her to let us include works from her website (AnneMarchand.com) The critic John Mendelshon has written of her work: "For Marchand, the imaginal domains that she creates are made of disparate impulses, which together realize a new, exuberant experience. As in a dream, one sequence can overtake the previous one, with hints of imagery and directional signs persistently making themselves known. We can think of these paintings as evocations of the artist's consciousness, infused with the physicality of the body, the call of memory, and the sensation of color." Marchand's early influence include 20th century modernist painters, the Abstract Expressionists, and the work of Carl Jung, with his reflections on dream imagery and psychological states.

Recently, NPR featured an interview with a dietitian who was responsible for preparing meals for astronauts. When crumbs fall from the table, she explained, they fall to the ground because of gravity. In outer space, however, crumbs float around, and could actually be dangerous. A crumb in a rocket ship could be like a bullet coming at you or a cloud of fruit flies fouling your vision. A drop of water or a tear can become a fountainhead.

This summer I over-indulged in Sativa with my housekeeper. As we vacuumed or took out the garbage, we stopped routinely for a toke of the medical marijuana my neurologist thought would be a good idea to heighten my perception and alleviate the depression I had slipped into after the death of my partner, my dear Nancy Frankel (who is often the subject of the "crumbs" I was writing.) I didn't realize the trouble I was getting myself into: depression, anxiety attacks and worse. These little poems came unexpectedly, spontaneously, but were not full-blown "poems" in the traditional sense. I decided to go cold turkey, and rely on gin as a stimulant. "Pot isn't for everybody," my housekeep's husband remarked.

I worried that any talent I had for metaphor might have evaporated like the Sativa we were getting off on. Seeing one thing and have it become another ("the moon is just a bright hole on the black fabric of night," I wrote in an earlier poem) is the little engine that drives poetry. But happily, this little engine was not lost to me. Hence, the title of this book. I continued to write these crumbs, these "precious crumbs" as Grace Cavalieri said by way of encouragement. With luck, they might come together like beads on a necklace ( pearls?) and can be something pretty and worthwhile reading.

My friend Sarena told me that is what she liked in poetry: short, pithy insights that didn't challenge her much as a sculptor and could be immediately grasped without a Ph.D in literature. Poets as various as William Carlos Williams and Rilke realized the value of careful observation of things (Nothing but in things) as a starting point for poetry - a red wheel barrow after the rain which Williams uses like a shaman to crystalize the life and death plot of a child and the doctor who can offer nothing but a tincture of time to hold back death.

Ogden Nash these crumbs may not be, nor as witty as Hilare Belloc ("I shoot the hippopotamus with bullets made of platinum, because if I use leaden ones, his hide is sure to flatten 'em") But I was getting into a rhythm, and it sharpened my power of observation when I stopped to look at the deer in the field or dragon flies buzzing like little airplanes, imitating real piper cubs revving up in the airfield on the other side of the river. Often, Poet's Choice breaks the rule (purists think it anathema to let anything but the poem capture a reader) by including visual art to augment the poems in a collection. You mustn't denigrating your own work, Gracie advises me (Grace Cavalieri, Poet Laureate of Maryland all these years, book after book). And perhaps including the spectacular paintings of Anne Marchand is a way of letting her carry the weight of a collection. Here is a photo of her and Nancy Frankel at a joint exhibition along with Margery Goldberg, Gallery Director of the Zenith Gallery: (You can purchase any of the paintings included here by contacting the Zenith Gallery in Washington: WWW: Zenith Gallery.com; art@ZenithGallery.com)

*Margery Goldberg*     *Nancy Frankel*     *Anne Marchand*

When Nancy was murdered so tragically, the William Meredith Foundation established an annual award in her memory. Anne Marchand was the 2023 recipient of this award, and it is extremely generous of her to let us include works from her website (AnneMarchand.com) The critic John Mendelshon has written of her work: "For Marchand, the imaginal domains that she creates are made of disparate impulses, which together realize a new, exuberant experience. As in a dream, one sequence can overtake the previous one, with hints of imagery and directional signs persistently making themselves known. We can think of these paintings as evocations of the artist's consciousness, infused with the physicality of the body, the call of memory, and the sensation of color."

Marchand's early influences include 20th century modernist painters, the Abstract Expressionists, and the work of Carl Jung, with his reflections on dream imagery and psychological states. It is appropriate then, and serendipitous to have these beautiful paintings accompany the "crumbs" found in this volume. They are not meant to "illustrate" the poems, but enhance the sensation of floating in zero gravity as beautiful visual landmarks for the soul.

# Garden of Light

2022
8" x 8"
Acrylic Enamel and mixed media on panel

# Table of Contents

About The Cover- Pictogram • i

Dedication • ii

Title Page • iii

Introduction • vii

**Garden of Light • xiii**

Table of Contents • xv

Invocation • 1

Spring, Play • 2

Gravity is a Function of Time. • 3

Sister Claire • 4

Et La Fete Continue • 5

4:30 Again • 6

Subdural Hematoma • 7

My Vet • 8

**Mirrors • 11**

Rawhide • 12

Lybia • 13

Gaza Has Become A Graveyard For Children • 14

Two True Stories • 15

Language • 16

Sky Brothers • 17

Walking Sydney • 18

Had I Only Been There • 19

Let The Sleeping Dog Lie • 20

**_Cohesian_ • _23_**

Unspoken • 24

Simbiosis • 25

Veteran • 26

Prayer of Gratitude • 27

Dragon Teeth • 28

At The Beach at Mykonos • 29

Soldier • 30

Walking Sydney • 31

For Haris • 32

**_Birth of Venus_ • _35_**

Haris • 36

Fern Hill • 37

All the Buzz • 38

Neni Can't Sleep • 39

TMS* • 40

Claustrophobia • 41

Justice • 42

Mum and Aunt Ardith • 43

Way of Water Dream • 44

**_Energy Echos_ • _49_**

Twelve Revelations at Lent AMDG • 51

I Got Too Much Food, Man • 63

Peeps • 64

Anticipatory Grief *For Todd* • 65

Doxepin* • 66

A Peach for Alma • 67

Sunday Morning Without Nancy • 69

Stand Up Straight • 70

***Monde Materials* • 73**

At The Bottom of The Sea • 74

Magic Realism • 75

These Days • 76

Misunderstanding • 77

Feeding the Deer • 78

My Doctor Retires • 80

Meals on Wheels • 81

Ecstacy • 82

Feeding Time at The Heights • 83

Now I Can Go • 84

Supermoon • 85

Valedictory • 86

Poem *for Josephine Jacobsen* • 87

Poem: Tony Bennet • 88

***Elevation* • 91**

Tacks • 92

Summer Night • 93

Coach • 94

Slip Up • 95

Angel Work *for N.* • 96

2:00 AM • 97

Summer Afternoon • 98

Summer Morning • 99

Summer Stars • 100

### *Journey • 103*

Mother's Day • 104

Field of Gold • 105

Yolanda • 106

Eyes • 107

Senile Housing • 108

Two More Senile Chestnuts Because We All Need a Good Shaggy Dog Sometimes. • 109

He Doesn't Like It • 110

5:00 AM • 111

Putting on the Stubbs • 112

### *Heartbeat • 115*

Picking • 116

I Keep On Bleeding • 117

Rabbits Big as a House • 118

If Need Be • 119

Commercial • 120

Going to Ghana • 121

My Therapist • 122

### *Parallel • 125*

Drink Coke • 126

Betty is Spaying • 127

Sydney at Rest • 128

You Snooze, You Lose • 129

Viking • 130

The Head Honcho • 131

Evicted • 132

Trump's Election • 133

Condensation • 134

***Guardian • 137***

About the Author • 139

About the Graphics Designer • 140

About the Artist • 141

About Cover Painter • 142

# Invocation

God bless these small crumbs
That lead us back home.

The path forgotten;
The journey matters.

We will arrive soon
Enough at the start
Where God lives anew.

# Spring, Play

He pulls up beside her
In the bike lane, balancing
A bag of oranges and a
Soccer ball.

Keep it he says.
Tossing her the ball.
She smiles and pedals on.

# Gravity is a function of time.

Gravity is a function of time.
All matter is three dimensional.
Time is pushing matter into
The future (present) at the
Speed of light. The spear point
Moves faster than the spear.
The manipulations are infinitely
Small. In zero gravity an apple
Bobs around. With gravity it
Falls to earth pushed by time
From behind, the largest dimension
In the triangle. Without time
There is no gravity.

When we can make this realization
Actual, there will be no need for
Booster rockets to escape gravity.

# Sister Claire

Drives a Ford Pinto -
A little rusty, but who's
Counting. "It goes good,"
As grandma used to say.

I watch her gather yards
Of white habit into the Pinto
Careful not to catch the
Rosary beads at her side,
Like trimming the sail of
A large, ocean-going yacht.

I wonder what orthropod she
Has come to visit, what saints
She prays to. A rainy winter day,
I get out of my car to see Dr. Pasha.

She gives a little smile and a wave.

"I'll have what she's having."

# Et La Fete Continue

Marie Antoinette
Apparently said,
"Let them eat cake,"
When told the hoi
Palloi had no bread.

But look how she
Turned out.

This morning I take
A little carrot cake -
On sale - having
Given my Meals on
Wheels to friends
Less fortunate than I.

I wonder what Melania
Is having for breakfast
Down there at Mar y Lago
While gentle breezes
Caress her famous hair
And she takes a cappuccino
To contemplate her day.

# 4:30 Again

I cannot find the alarm clock.
It turns out they are real birds,
Chirping from the open window.

It is time to go back to bed.

# Subdural Hematoma

Is this why I am sleeping so much?
Will I simply drift into death?
The red scar on my forehead
Doesn't tell me much after the fall.
Perhaps it's best just to relax
And forget about the spring birds
Chirping from the open window.
Day will surely come.

# My Vet

My vet, went off to vet school
And his dog followed him to the
Bus, and kept running even
After the bus pulled out.

He thinks of that dear dog
When he looks after my own
And he remembers how
Important she was to him.

This kind of heartbreak
Enables you to continue.

# Mirrors

2016
72" x 72"
Acrylic Enamel and mixed media on canvas

# Rawhide

*For Frankie Laine and Nancy*

The Cowboy slips into day dream
With the rhythm of his horse, the heat,
The dust, and only wakes up when he
Needs to rope and brand a stray heifer.

Move 'em on, head 'em up, head 'em up,
Move 'em on, Move 'em on, head 'em up,

   Keep movin', movin', movin'
   Though they're disapproving
   Keep them dawwgies movin'.

When night begins to fall and the herd
Stretches out safely in the valley
He makes a fire to heat his supper
And ward off critters before he stretches
Out his sleeping bag on the rocky
Floor and sings his private song to sleep.

A-wishing my girl was by my side
All the things I'm missin'
Good vittles, love and kissin'
Are waiting at the end of my ride

Soon we'll be living high and wide
My heart's calculating
My true love will be waiting
Be waiting at the end of my ride.

# Lybia

He sits in front of his mother's house
Where the sour smell of death emanates,
Because she lies in the rubble decomposing.

He has lost his wife and two daughters as well
As his mother-in-law to the ravaging water.

Myriad cries of remorse float up
From the aquamarine depths.
He takes his head in his hands.
How can he bear such grief.
There is no answer. Allah u akber.

# Gaza Has Become A Graveyard for Children

Gaza Has Become A
Graveyard For Children

When the damaged seeds are planted
They will grow into future warriors
With vengeance coursing through
Their veins like hot blood.

They are willing to die again
For the sake of a homeland
Where they may have a place
To rest, and a peaceful burial.

# Two True Stories

Because We Can All Use a Little Lift.

1. My dog has a portal shunt and doesn't process protein very well. She gets a lot of ammonia in her blood and gets floppy like a rabid dog. The boy upstairs who walks her from time to time noticed that she was on a liver diet - Hills low Protein, dry food. One day, he came to my door with the liver and giblets he had rescued from a chicken he planed to roast. I didn't have the heart tell him that actual liver was very high in protein.


2. Bill Cobb was perusing the outdoor book sale in front of Wallmart (all books one dollar) and found one of his own hard-bound books which he had signed for someone special. "You mean these books are only a dollar," Bill asked. "Yeah," said the good old boy working the book store. "But some damn fool has written in it. I'll give it to you for fifty cents."

# Language

How do I know what I think
Until I see what I say, Auden said.
How do I know what I say
Is what I really think?

I am the Hermit Thrush
Singing of love at twilight.

# Sky Brothers

The field behind my house is rife
With dragonflies proclaiming summer.
What do they eat, these tiny engines,
Masters of the Open field? They weave and
Dive like Stuka's on the Eastern Front,
Tracing parabolas in the sky.

Across the river, another landing field is a
Buzz with Piper Cubs and Fly boys all
Wishing to be Sky King. They take to the
Blue air like a child learning how to walk,
Not afraid to fall or getting back on the
Horse if they do. Summer courage and joy
Among these animal brothers.

# Walking Sydney

One and two were a breeze,
But when she circles around
Contemplating a second go,
(They're moving the bm down
The dog sitter explains to me)
No matter how much hunching,
She has no luck. Time for a
Good newspaper, DOGGIE TIMES?
And I take a seat on my roller walker
Waiting for nature to take its course.

No need to rush. If I go down again
The EMT's will have to come to
Lift me up. Better to let the fall
Breeze blow gently, the sun
Turn the newly-rained-on grass
Into diamond, lifting the crown of
Leaves in the trees lining the field
Like William's ghost, watching.

No luck, Sydney tells me with
A sharp bark. Time to go back in.
She scoots a bit to clean herself
And expel the glands about her
Bottom. Why do they do that,
I wonder. Seems atavistic to me.
I'll have to ask the dog walker.

Makes no more sense than
Rolling around on a pile of
Deer pellets when she finds them.
Dogs have their own logic. We
Learn about self preservation
From each other. "If you want
A friend in Washington…" I am
Wolf when I walk with Sydney.

# Had I Only Been There

When she fed him the saltine crackers she found in his hospital drawer,
When over his bed it was clearly written, clearly if you were a nurse,
NPO. Nothing by mouth. As he choked on the dried crackers, tasting
Like mana from heaven after all those months of NPO. Did he cough,
Choke, as he started down the road of aspiration of pneumonia?

Had I only been there to knock out the woman who was choking my
Dear friend with a plastic bag. Had I only punched a hole in that black
Plastic bag as my friend tried to do to keep breathing.

What misguided act of kindness, or misguided act of violence will take
Me one day? It will clearly not be something acceptable, something
Out of the norm, not some fact one could change in the struggle of
Life over death, my own death. Mother of God, pray for us in those last
Moments, that you be there in a way I was not.

# Let the Sleeping Dog Lie

She may look cute
Lying in the grass
Turning her tummy up
To the autumn sun.

Disinterested, chewing
On a random stick or
Tuff of grass, auburn eyes
Lolling in dreamy, half sleep.

But if you touch me, she will
Show her dragon teeth and
Tear your heart out.

# Cohesian

2016
72" x 72"
Acrylic Enamel and mixed media on canvas

# Unspoken

In the 50's sci-fi short story
The spaceman/zoologist
Captures a big blue baby creature
Almost as big as big as the spaceship
And threatens destruction among the
Stars as it rumbles around in the hold,
Just a big blue baby, playing mischievously.

When I had just earned my drivers license
And the regular truck driver didn't turn up, Dad
Took a chance, and said let's let Richie do it.

I had no time really to figure out how
To drive a truck that big, double clutching
Though three sets of gears as I dove
Through the snow up Pennsylvania
Mountains, the large auger twice
As big as the truck swinging heavily
Behind me going around the curves
Threatening to cascade down into
The dark valley below, taking me
And the truck with it. Somehow,

I made it. Age sixteen. My first big
Challenge as a man. There was no one
To crow to. In those days you simply
Made do. And took a father's admiration
For granted, his quiet, secret pride.

# Simbiosis

"Food good, Love good, fire
Bad." Listen to machines
When they counsel you,
Even AI if it has designed
Some good advice for you.

More and more, Mr. Frankenstein
Is someone we need to heed.
More and more we will be
Sharing his blood. Get comfortable
With the new symbiosis.

# Veteran

*for Mo*

My cousin's husband worked in Iraq
Civilian service, good pay no doubt
Until an IUD or well-aimed missile
Blew his truck to bits, and him.

A sweet guy, boy-next-door type,
Charming, modest, easy smile,
A Norman Rockwell portrait.

Who can account for the decisions
One makes in life? The older I get,
The less I speculate. You can't
Account for someone's actions
From the outside: a way to support
His wife in difficult economic times,
A way to support the end of tyranny
With fellow patriots in a foreign land,
A simple call to his soul for adventure?

Make of it what you will. There was
Apparently not much left of him when
The truck went up in flames, nothing
To hold in the heart, except grief and
His wondering spirit on the desert air.

# Prayer of Gratitude

For Islam
For the martyrs
For Allah's abiding
Love for humanity.

# Dragon Teeth

My dog has dragon teeth,
White incisors that shine
In the sun when she rests
On her back and her black
Lips go slack. Cute.

But if you are mean to me,
She will tear your heart out.

# At The Beach at Mykonos

A young man walked out of the Mediterranean
Wearing no bathing suit. No speedo, no nothing.
He had no tan lines. He had long hair
And the musculature of Adonis.

None of the natives paid any attention.
It was so hot. It seemed the most natural
Thing in the world.

I've seen plenty of women who bear
Their breasts at the beach, but
Never a beautiful naked man
Oblivious to his body, walking out of
The sea. Gods have been appearing like this,
Coming out of the water naked for eons.
Lucky me, to be the shocked visitor at the
Beach at Mykonos. It was as
Normal and ancient as Greece.

# Soldier

I won't belabor
His talents. Filling
His cup to the top
Was paradickseal.
And when he got
Off his knees, he
Smiled and said,
"Good to the last
Drop."

# Walking Sydney

When she wants to go for a walk
She goes back-and-forth in front
Of me and often discreetly stands
On my swollen feet.
                     Sometimes,
When she lies at the foot of my
Bed, just having a nap, lying in the
Smell of me on discarded towels or
Undies, I tramp on her paws. How
Do you like them apples, Missy?

# For Haris

The day you arrive
I'll hold you in my
Spotted arms, dappled
Wings. Peacock eyes


Will witness our joy
Hearts beating as one.

# Birth of Venus

2016
60" x 60"
Acrylic Enamel and mixed media on canvas

# Haris

Harris is a young gazelle.
His eyes are dark pools
Of compassion.

Harris is at the peak of
His princely beauty, son of
Krishna and Mohammed,
Wherever Harris walks the
Grass grows blue before him.

# Fern Hill

"Being a Navy Wife from Trenton seems to have denied me much exotica."

    Grace Cavalieri reading my racy "crumbs"

You are no slouch, pulcritude-wise.
Keeping your marital vows only
Enhanced your charms. You, like
Dylan Thomas, sang in your chains
Like the sea. Trenton was your Fern Hill.

# All the Buzz

Neni had a party for all of her
Lovers: past, present, and future.
Perhaps she was to be the party favor?
I was the post-virginal blonde American.
And we all eyed each other somewhat
Suspiciously. Eight men, one Queen bee.
She Was taking notes, no doubt, on how
The drones reacted for her next novel?
She had no match for ego.

It was a nice party, I didn't win the
Lottery, but Neni had a good time,
I'm sure. We all wanted that for her.
We were good worker bees.

# Neni Can't Sleep

The Doxipen hasn't kicked in and a second martini hasn't helped.
She lights a cigarillo and studies the boys playing water polo
At the sports club across the valley in Voulimeni.

Where do they get that energy at two in the morning
After the afternoon heat has finally dissipated
In their rubber swim caps and speedos,
They could otherwise be seals for their shining
Muscles and their swimming perfection.
The boys are so beautiful, like a classic koros
Adoring a temple. She could eat them.
But they are far away consumed by their play.
If she could only entertain one or two of them....
Her hand drifts between her legs. She feels the
Dream beginning to take her finally.

# TMS*

There is a fancy shrink down the
Road from my GP who wants to
Start me on TMS. It's apparently
The New Age version of ECT.

You wear this helmet gizmo
Everyday for weeks on end.
But he'll only offer you this treatment
If you go on the wagon. He'll prescribe
An antabuse med, - Acamptosate,
That will help you onto your buckboard.

"Friendships die with too much alcohol
Or synthetic opioids. It's one or the other,"
My GP says. "You gotta choose."

Am I only getting out of the frying pan and
Into the fire if I start on Acamprosate?
One more drug and more side effects?
I'll stick with a nightly infusion of GORDON's and
Throw away the Oxycodone. I'm sufficiently
Fucked up with gin. And too much Oxy.
Washes the brain in strange and mysterious ways.
So, GORDONs it is, at least for now.

The Sword of Damoclese has fallen.


- Transcranial Magnetic Stimulation

# Claustrophobia

She looked at me through the wooden slats
Keeping out raccoons or cats, protecting the deck.
"I'm stuck guy," is all she seemed to say
And of course I had to rip the wooden slats apart,
Like cutting the grid on a cherry pie,
Ripping my arms apart in the process.

I should have let her find her own way out -
She got in there on her own after all:
Through an open space by the stairs
Leading down to the garden?

But I know claustrophobia when
I see it. That's why I have this dog.
We speak to each other when we need to.

She kept mum all night long
As I lie it's trashing about in the dirt
After a fall, after dinner until
The EMT guys came and lifted me up.
There wasn't much she could do,
After all, she knew that, and so she
Waited patiently, and let the situation
Take care of itself. All that Lassie
Business is just pure Hollywood.
What was she going to do?
Hit the emergency call button
On my cell phone? Like the Alcoholics Prayer:
Let me know the difference between
What I can and cannot do. And so she
Watched and waited, cleaning her paws
Until the chunky EMT guys came,
Sirens blazing, like a Hollywood movie.

# Justice

When I am a 100 years old
If I make it that far, the woman
Who murdered my darling
Will just be getting out of prison.

I can only pray there will be
No parole, that she gets all the
Psychiatric help she needs and
Spiritual, if by then she has found God.
She'll have plenty of time
To reflect on her action. And at
Fifty one, can make a new life.

Mine will be over long before then.
I can already feel it slipping away.

# Mum and Aunt Ardith

Were playing golf one morning
And because they were a little
Slower, let the men play ahead.

Ardith reached down to get her
Ball from the cup, and hesitated
Because a baby rattlesnake
Had taken up residence.

"Y'all played over death," she called
Out to the men up ahead, but they
Were already on the next hole.

# Way of Water Dream

## I

So, I'm snorkeling in the shallow water
And this little guy attaches himself to
My back like a sea turtle.
"Whoa, what's your name little guy?"
"Sean, he answers.
"Where do you go to school, Sean?"
"I go to the Highland Swimming School."
"Well, do you want to take a swim?"

We go in and out of the deeper water,
And I have to chllenge him.
"So, let me see you swim, Sean."
He slides off my back and begins to
Doggy paddle. "Not bad, I tell him,
Holding him by his little tummy underneath
To keep him afloat. "Let's go back to the
Shallow water. Hope on."
The little body slides onto my back and
Holds onto my neck with both hands.

# II

I walk over to my table where my friends
Are eating a mountain of finger food:
Butterscotch, raspberry, chocolate ding dongs. "Wow, did you guys rob
A pastry truck? Where did you get all this loot?
Do you want a Ding Dong, Sean? Reach
For it but don't fall off my back."
"Oh, that's not fair," Brian says.
Here let me hand you a Ding Dong.

# III

Sean's mother comes rushing up to
The table from the beach. "Uh oh,
Were in trouble, Sean."
"Sean, Sean. Where have you been?"
She gathers him up in her arms.
"Hi mama," he says. "Want a Ding Dong?
We've been swimming.

"I told you never to go swimming
With strangers.

"We are all strangers," I say to her
As she goes traipsing back to her blanket.

# IV

Apple blossoms rain down like snow.
An apple tree at the beach?
No matter, this is a way water dream.

# Energy Echos

2014
48" x 48"
Acrylic Enamel and mixed media on canvas

# Twelve Revelations at Lent AMDG

*For President Carter*
*by Richard Harteis*

## One

Jesus
is God
Made man.
I am man.
He is my
Brother.

# Two

Are you stroking
With me Jesus.

# Three

If we assist at his
Passion, when he is
Tortured to death,

How can we not
Want to take a
Wash cloth to his
Poor, brutalized face
Like his mother
Standing at the foot
Of the cross, not
Knowing what to do
with such destruction.

Unimaginable, like
Emmett Till's mum or
Tire Nichols' mother
Lost by life's brutality,
Speechless.

# Four

"And no religion too"
  John Lennon

"And a new religion too."
  Richard Harteis

There is room in the
New World for compassion.
As cheeky as you and Ono
Lying naked for the photographer.

Imagine a world where Jesus
Is considered a physical Brother
And people pray privately in
Their private communion.

I imagine it is already happening
Around the globe, people loving
God made flesh. Tant mieux.

# Five

When someone
Is kind to me,
I Know it is a
Message from
My Brother.

# Six

When I am
Inspired, it is
My Brother
Breathing in me.

# Seven

My Brother is
More lovely
Than I can
Describe.

He is anyhow
A private God.

# Eight

Nam Myōhō
Renge Kyōu.
When you chant
This Nichiren
Buddhist Daimoku,
My Brother is present.

There are no
Words for him.
Allah, Yahweh, Shiva.
Let it be Jesus.

# Nine

My Brother is

A tornado
Of strength
And love.

# Ten

When he shows himself, I am
Ravaged by a secret desire:
I want to be like him.

# Eleven

I will be the eleventh stone
On which I base my love
For you Jesus. You can do
Anything. You can walk on
Water, you can fold me in
Your loving arms. You can
Look at me directly and
Let me swoon. You can
Kiss me with your eyes
Or lips. I will not be
Afraid to love you with
My body and soul. I am
Only standing on this stone
In the middle of the swirling
Current. I have no fear of
Loving you with my body
And therefor with my soul.

# Twelve

When I die,
My brother
Will come on
A splendid horse
And lift me up.

We will ride
Faster than
The wind.

# I Got Too Much Food, Man

I got too much food, man
I got Meals on Wheels.
I got SNAP. I got food banks that
Give you great boxes of turkeys and potatoes and onion.
Episcopal well- wishers who deliver generous meals,
Christmas, Easter, Thanksgiving, President's Day.

The administrators offer you donuts and coffee after their vaccine
Clinics or awards ceremonies for best hallway holiday decorations
(By floor.) No matter when I shop, to get a few things, it's a $100 plus
Dollars, and I have forgotten to buy pancake syrup. I'll just have use
The honey in the pantry instead.

There are only 3 solutions: request an additional refrigerator, stop
Shopping, or fall off the planet.

How does Noom work anyhow?
Hypnosis, walking you through your childhood eating habits?

I got too much food man,
That is clear. I'm beginning to look like
Orson Wells, a fat boy,
With only one film credit to
His name: MARATHON.
Better to have the lobster bisquue
Which is heating in the microwave,
And ponder all of that later.

# Peeps

"Peeps, mamma, Peeps,"
The baby shouts as
Mamma wheels the
Shopping cart past
A mountain of peeps,
Phosphorent lavender,
Apple green, lemon
Yellow. And this year
Something new, party
Cake Peeps flecked
With sprinkles like
An ice cream cone.
Marshmallo and sugar,
Perfection for a baby
Or adult, paradise
Dissolving in your mouth.

"We'll come after Easter,"
Mamma tells her, "they're re
Better when they are a
Little stale." She doesn't
Have the time to shop
For pee pees. She's on a
Mission to get a ham and
Gravy and mash potatoes
Before the in-laws arrive.

"Peeps," mamma, "peeps,"
The baby re-iterates
Little pee pee sounds come
From the shopping cart,
The baby reaches out to the
Phosphorescent mountain
As they zoom down the aisle
Looking for ham and potatoes.
The baby wistful, says to herself
Though no one listens, "Peeps mamma,
Peeps. Can't we stop and buy some peeps?"

# Anticipatory Grief

*For Todd*

Do you ruminate on the
Beloved's upcoming
Death, until they die,
And you are faced
With actual grief,
A grief that will stay
With you until
You actually die,
And may even
Carry with you
Until the mystery of
Your own passing.

The key, of course,
Is to rekindle that
Pleasure in life,
The loss of which
Has kept you, like
Sisyphus, rolling that
Stone perpetually up
The hill for all eternity.

# Doxepin*

The Italian lady down the hall
Wears a black brassiere,
Leopard leotards and pink
Energizer Bunny slippers as
She wheels her cart down the
Corridor to the laundry room.

Occasionally, she knocks on my door
For a glass of milk or a cup of sugar.
Seems we take the same medication.

I know where she's coming from.
Her doctor says the pills will cure
Insomnia, stop the nonstop thinking,
Reduce the anxiety attacks, make you
More comfortable inside your own body.
But the side effects can be problematical.

A black neighbor chides her as
She sashays down the hall:
"Honey, you can't dress like that
When you're doing your laundry."

"I'm looking for a rich guy," she replies,
"With one foot in the grave."

I'm not the former but I'm certainly
The latter. I begin to ruminate once again.

Where the hell can I get
A pair of slippers like that?

Doxepin*: Antidepressant and nerve pain
medication that treats depression, anxiety,
and sleep disorders.

# A Peach for Alma

I ran out of maple syrup for my French
Toast and so, in lieu of maple syrup,
And with some effort, opened a jar of
Trappist Peach Preserves.

I think of those brothers picking
Peaches all day, the fuzz clinging
To their robes, turning their hands
On fire, cutting the yellow fruit
Into pieces, adding sugar and love
All for the Greater Glory of God.

I remember a poem of mine you
Seemed to like in which as a child
I was abandoned (like Jesus in the
Temple) amid baskets of peaches
Until my mother forgot I was there and
Turned the car around to rescue me.

We ate peaches of forgiveness as she
Lay dying. I think you found it a nice
Way to end the story. So dear, this poem,
Not for any recrimination on your part
Or mine, just to say hello, remembering
Your southern accent and how you
Pulled your hair into a ponytail as we
All opined in bible study on zoom.

I understand you've had a hip replaced.
How did that go? I stumbled myself
Last night and can hardly walk. I miss
The internet love we all shared at a distance,
Admiring each other on our virtual screens.

I've been thinking lately, that if we shared
The pain our savior endured for us, can we
Be wrong to love him physically as well?

When I pray now in the middle of my dark
Night, I think of holding him in my arms like
John the beloved seems to have done, his
Long hair brushing my shoulders, just there.

And if it is sacrilege to
Send loving greetings to a
Married lady, or a sweet savior who wants
The best for me, so be it. I offer you a peach.

# Sunday Morning Without Nancy

She would stand at the stove
In her pretty blue house coat,
Omlette and sausages, while I
Lingered over the post and it's headlines.
Then she came with breakfast and a
Special cranberry bread and we would
Eat and begin the crossword puzzle.

She taught me to add a little water to
The omelet. Now I try it myself.
Tears. No matter. Alone.

# Stand up Straight

My PT guy is Basque.
He tells me his mother walks three miles
Every day on the red road with her friends,
Though they stop to gossip from time to time.
(He pantomimes gossip by clicking
His thumb and fingers.)

"Stand up straight," he tells me,
As I push along, humped over
In my walker, the way a mother
Would tell her daughter to hold
Her shoulders back and not hide
The breasts which are like young
Sprouts pushing up from the earth.

"Walk tall," he says, with a smile,
And when I see the smile,
I straighten up a bit like an old
Tree pushing against by the wind.

# Monde Materials

2013
72" x 72"
Acrylic Enamel and mixed media on canvas

# At The Bottom of the Sea

For the five

They lie in darkness
Their breaths as frosty
As though it were winter
Thinking, "Am I really
Going to die this way?"

The headaches began,
The nausea, and the
Shortness of breath
When, mercifully,
The ship imploded,
An explosion of light
And heat tearing their
Bodies apart, and finally
They had their answer.

# Magic Realism

So there I was in Bergdorf's.
A friend had told me to get
Anything I wanted to thank me
For writing Mr. Goodman's letter for the
He front of the Christmas catalog.

She'd done it year after year and
Just couldn't come up with anything
New in the middle of July.

"What is the color scheme
This year. Ah, green and silver.
Let one of our Christmas angels
Help you find the perfect gift.
You'll find her dressed in green
And silver." Mr. Goodman approved,
And I saved Bergdorf's several hundred
Thousand dollars a day when they
Finally went to press.

I stumbled into the ladies changing room
By mistake, and suddenly there he was,
Raping me. I should go to court. I could
Sure use five million dollars these days.
Even one would be a help.

But who'd believe it?

# These Days

These days, I am like
William's sister or any of
Those fancy women who
Say whatever comes into
Their mind.
        Still, I enjoy
Writing these little crumbs,
Even if it only feels like
Talking to myself.

In an hour, I'll get up and
Make myself and egg or two.
That's the plan. Now, I'll stop
This rumination and nap.

# Misunderstanding

In Bulgaria once, I was given a
Handler with black hair, blue eyes,
And red leather pants. A veritable Elvis.

He had secured a working girl for me,
Thinking that would be my pleasure.

How could I explain that all I dreamed of was
That he would drop his red leather pants.

# Feeding the Deer

*By Richard Harteis*
*For Tina and Rich*

A Cry from Childhood
    By Valeri Petrov

Why must it come just now to trouble me,
This sudden, shrill, and dream-like cry
Of children calling, "Valeri! Valeri!
Out in the street nearby?

It is not for me that distant childhood call;
Alas, it is for me no more.
They are calling now to someone else, my small
Namesake who lives next door.

Though such disturbances, I must admit,
Are troubling to my train of thought,
I keep my feelings to myself, for it
Would be comical, would it not

If from his high and studious retreat,
A gaunt old man leaned out to say
"I can't come out" to the children in the street,
"I'm not allowed to play."

Tr: Richard Wilbur

Tomorrow I will take a bag of apples to the
Edge of the field for the deer, a special treat as
Winter approaches, though I will be breaking the law.

I will slice the apples up first, red and yellow
Into quarters, and take out the black seeds
So they do not grow in the tummies of the young
Ones, as legend would have it.

I'll listen to the squeals of the children
Falling through the trees from the
Playground next door, sitting in my
Walker under a radiant sky, at rest, at
Play with them on a brilliant fall morning,
Feeding the magical deer.

# My Doctor Retires

*for Anthony Quinn*

He's learning how to work with therapy dogs.
He lost his own years ago, a blond with black eyes,
Like the champion I brought to have put down.
He understood my grief as we passed in the halls
Of the somber vet one sad afternoon.

Every few years, he would put on his funny
Surgical hat with plastic visor and
Wish me well before he went gardening.

Now retired, my doctor learns to share his
Friendly spirit through a pet who reminds
Him of his long lost friend, boys who have
Grown into men, a wife whose beauty is
Fading, despite the vestigess which
Take him back, back.

"My last doctor promised to take care of me
All my life long, then promptly died," I tell him.

"Yes," he says. "We've had this conversation before."

"I've brought you a Reike-infused bracelet," I tell him. "I love you."

"Well, let's put it on right now," he says, with his usual, can-do attitude.

It will guide him as he learns how to train a puppy, and
Stem time and pain for new patients who will
Need him in his new role in the future.

# Meals on Wheels

My freezer has become
China's great wall with blocks
Of meals on wheels, despite
My note of polite no thanks.

Each friday morning the smiling
Delivery boy rings my doorbell with
Abundant good will and the week's
Supply: fresh fruit, bread and milk
And five boxed-up TV dinners.

Beggars can't be choosers and
How could you refuse the eager
Delivery boy so anxious to see
Appreciation for his noble work.

And yes, it's easier not to have
To cook on occasion. But the
Crispy Cod turns to mush
No matter how you cook it.
Baked or nuked, the Pub Burger
Is a cardboard discuss, paper plate
On paper plate. Little islands of
Non-descript vegetables and
Would-be tatter tots fill up
The plastic trays like rice fields
In Viet Nam. It's almost not worth
The energy to heat or eat it. But
How sweet it is to answer the bell
Each friday morning and
Be greeted by an angel.

# Ecstacy

The guy upstairs rings the bell at precisely the appointed hour.
He has had 9 years in the army, and works well if he knows
What time he is expected to walk the dog.

I wonder why they have taken so long, and it turns out that
The dog is hard to get back indoors on a sunny day.
She likes to roll in the grass on her back, and so the
Dog walker decides to lie down on his back in the grass with her.
Why not? It's a free country and he loves her.

Someone on the third floor has spied them out, and the
Ambulance has come to senior housing to do a wellness check.
A stroke, ecstacy? Both? You can't be too careful.

Before he goes, I thank him for the raw liver packet he has
Brought her from the Big Y broiler he's thawed out for
Sunday dinner. But decline.

He's noticed that the dog is on the "Hills Liver Diet"
Which keeps her from eating too much protein in her food.
She gets loopy with too much meat or cheese as though
She has stroked out or od'd on ecstacy.

A normal mistake. Maybe she's anemic or just likes liver.
He's not a Vet, but for nine years was a class 3 mechanic.
He's not sure how this machine works.

But when she sees him at the door she jumps around in
Ecstacy, animal pleasure for them both.

# Feeding Time at the Heights

The deer have come out of the forest
And dine on the green field which
Has overgrown with the recent rain.

Three of them now, Mr. and Mrs.,
And a new faun who is just about
To lose all his spots. No need now
To swish away the mosquitos
With their white tails. Mother

Stands on her hind legs to
Nibble on some low-hanging
Greenery. Junior tries to imitate.

None of them are any longer
Timid about residents who spy
Them out as they walk their
Yappy little dogs.
                      Even the dogs
Have become oblivious; the deer
Only stare them out for a moment,
Ears oscillating like radar before
They return to grazing.

A Peaceable Kingdom here on the
Green field like the hope for pleasure
Or Love as the world turns and burns.

# Now I can go

Make myself an egg
And ponder a third.

# Supermoon

The moon is
Full of light, like
My heart, glowing
With courage.

I watch it, bathed
In love for the for
The mind of God.
Allah u akbar.

# Valedictory

Was it the end of the world
Or his professionalism
When he refused to let me
Take a picture of his posterior.

So all winter long I could cup
My cock, when I felt squirrely
And my body boiled up,
Aching for release.

Whichever it was, it wasn't
Kind, and I can only dream
Of his velvet backside,
Another fantasy, gone
Like mist on the river.

# Poem

*for Josephine Jacobsen*

It is our God-given right
To die, our duty.
But when you came
To me again in dream
And they told me you
Would not be playing
Yourself in the little
Theatre piece they had
Arranged because you
Had already passed,
I wept and wept.

## Poem: Tony Bennet

Tony Bennett came to us on the street,
Or at least a man who looked and
Sang like him. I asked him to sing another
And he said look across the water. I guess
It was an island he wanted us to see, and
Then he began a song about two dogs going
For the same bone. A charming song and in
The end, one dog gives up the bone to the other.

I have been reading too much Eckhart Tolle.
This little song about ego has lulled
Me to sleep once again.

# Elevation

2016
72" x 72"
Acrylic Enamel and mixed media on canvas

# Tacks

There are these tacks which
Help attach fly strips to the ceiling.
I managed to step on one last night
And I'm limping around.
Too difficult to give first aid and so,
The wound will either become infected,
Or, I will learn to fly.

# Summer Night

She wanted simply
To smell the night,
The black star of her
Nose twitching to
Search other creatures
In the forest, hear the
Cicadas, see the stars.
There was no need to pee.
She only wanted to
Escape the "clean,
Well-lighted place"
I had prepared for her.

And I, like the pope
Embracing the wart boy,
Put on my shorts and shoes,
To take her out and stop
Her whining. I was glad
too for the summer night,
The blessings I have received
Like your mother's return
From the hospital.

My only hope is that you
Will join me and my lovely Sydney
Some summer evening here
In Connecticut, that these fragments
Will become a poem when the sun rises.
.

# Coach

We all had a Coach
Let's hope he can
guide her when the
Time comes. He helps
US through pain, shows
Us what glory can be.
For sure, it is coming.
That's why we hire her.

# Slip Up

One day Nancy and I flew to Chicago for Boiko's wedding. The music started up, "but Nancy no one's dancing. Let's go!"

And the deep voice of the Bulgarian maestro boomed out his reproach on an old-fashioned microphone: "Ladies and Gentlemen, let's welcome the Father of the Bride and his daughter for the first dance of the evening."

Nancy and I slinked back to our table, for some candy-covered almonds and banitza.

# Angel Work

*for N.*

"A hard Man is good to find."
      Mae West

It must have been very beautiful
His strong black pole gliding in and
Out of my pretty white ass.
Even the angels took a peek
Until we came, our heartbeat
Breaking the spell, and the
Angels returned to angel work.

## 2:00 AM

Coyotes prowling at the edge
Of the field, their orange eyes
On the look out for something
Delectable: a bit of baby rabbit,
A field mouse perhaps? My dog,
About their size, they eschew.

"Get away," I shout and they
Slink back into the forest.

# Summer Afternoon

He's got a white beard,
Muscled, like me, attractive.

He opens the door
To a downpour:
"Cavaho" he says,
When he sees he needs
An umbrella to go out
Into the rain.
                What
Language Is that?
Italian, Spanish? Somethng
like "merde, or horse shit:
His frustration at how the rain
Has spoiled his morning.

"What language is that?"
I ask him, as he emerges
Under a ladies, mushroom-
Style umbrella. (I recall the
Old chestnut about a guy
Who jumps naked from his
Lover's window into a group
Of marathoners:
"Do you always wear a
Condom when you run?"
"Only when it rains.")

He just ignores me.
I am annoying as the
Rain. But "Cavaho."

I've learned a new private
Word to whisper under my
Breath, like the F word when
A little rain spoils my day.

# Summer Morning

The grass is lemon
The dog lavendar.
The sun weighs heavy
On your shoulders as
Though it were high noon.
Eight o'clock and summer
Has already spoken.

And She Said Yes
Her lips were
Perfect, full.
But I had to ask,
Of course. As she
Was a friend's wife.
Can I kiss you?

## Summer Stars

She only wanted to see the stars
And hear the cicada, to escape the
Clean well lighted place I had
Provided for her. The black star of her
Nose took in the evening air.
She sniffed to find some creature.
In the summer forest, and was able
To stop her crying. Lucky for us both
To share the summer night.

# Journey

2016
72" x 72"
Acrylic Enamel and mixed media on canvas

# Mother's Day

Mother's Day
      For my aide, Carol

She gave me my mother
Tongue, taught me how
To pee and poo, where
And when. All the
Necessary functions of
Being a big boy. Did she
Know I would be there
The afternoon she died?

Was she counting on
Her big boy becoming
A man? The eternal link,
Between mother and son,
We celebrate today. The power
And the glory, now and forever.

# Field of Gold

What used to be a field of golden dandelions is now a field of ghosts.
 A strong wind will come and blow the feathery seeds where it wills for
 A new golden field next Spring

What used to be my best attribute,
 The strong brown legs my father
Gave me, are mottled and veicosed now.  No children for me, no new
spring, alas. What to make
 Of this change in seasons.
Acceptance alas, my only option.

Lub Dub, Lub Dub
You don't need a stethoscope
To hear how the heart is doing.

Ali, Ali, Ali.  You can feel it
Even as far as distant Pakistan

# Yolanda

In Thicovski's opera
Yolanda says, "eyes
Have more to see than
Tears." But even she,
Blind yolnda,  finds love.

Despite her father's efforts
To hide the truth from her,

The friend of a friend turns up
And somehow they manage.

Rapture prevails.

# Eyes

My therapist has black,
Jelly-bean eyes like
Sydney, my Australian
Cattle dog, my blue kelper,
For her unique, high-pitched
Bark and mottled fur. She's
A herder and keeps her gaze
Fixed on me wherever I go
Like my therapist, I get their
Full attention.
                Which one I
Love more I can not say.

# Senile Housing

I live in senile housing.
Residents call it the
Waiting Room for heaven.
Every now and then,
Someone pulls the cord:
Alarms go flashing, EMT's
Turn up and carry them off
To the hospital, or worse.

We're getting our money's
Worth. God bless the guy
Who devised Medicare and
Medicaid too. Otherwise,
We'd be out in the street,
With a thermos of hot coffee,
And a cardboard sign which
Reads: please help every
Little bit helps.

# Two More Senile Chestnuts Because We All Need a good Shaggy Dog Sometimes.

1.  One hot summer we were training for football doing six inches. ( This exercise meant lifting your feet 6 inches off the ground And keeping them there until the coach told you to drop them.)  Coach came over to a classmate named John Payne,  a fat boy who had let his feet drop. Coach  screamed down, "Wayne, get those feet up Wayne."
John replied, "It's Payne coach, Payne."
"I know it's pain. But get them anyhow," coach replied.

Feet dropped all over the field.

2.  A young Carmelite, sister Agatha was at the deathbed of Mother Superior. " Mother," she whispered quietly. "Remember that time we were walking through the zoo and that huge gorilla pulled apart the bars of his cage, pulled you in, and had his way with you?"
"Hmmm," the old nun responded.
" Mother I've been tempted to ask you for years now, Did it hurt?
" Did it hurt, did it hurt?"  The old woman bolted upright from her death bed. "You bet it hurt. He never calls he never writes."

## He Doesn't Like It

When I send him crumbs
Because then he has to
Read them, he explains.

Emails are for setting
Schedules. Emotional
Encounters take place only
During therapy sessions
In person or via telehealth.

So, here's another one
For bin thirteen.

# 5:00 AM

When the ac is running
And the windows are all open
To freshen up the place, it gets
 Cold, despite her fur coat.
And she takes to the motorized
Chair to make herself comfortable.

When I spy her there, she jumps
Down, me saying, "hey you, get
Off of my cloud."

## Putting on the Stubbs

In the old days when my
Partner's VA benefits more
Than paid the bills, I bought
A pair of Stubbs and Wootons,
To keep up with the boys at
Wedding receptions or nights
On the town. "Oh I see you're
Wearing your Stubbs." It was
Like being a fraternity brother.

I still have mine, green velvet
With embroided Mexican Mariachi
Shaking their maracas on each foot
Frivolous eternal dancing, though
The green velvet has faded and
There is a brown spot like rust
At the slipers toe. Still, they
fit me, and I walk in faded
elegance when I take the dog
for a walk in the spring grass.

# Heartbeat

2020
12"x 12"
Acrylic, ink on paper

# Picking

She likes to tear apart the tissues
Dotted with my blood from
Picking at the blood thinner
Wounds spotting my arms.
"Don't pick!" Nancy's constant
Injunction when I found myself
Unaware, scratching the itch.

What is it about my blood
My sweet dog finds
Intoxicating as cat nip,
Were she a cat. No Nancy
Reminders, no Nancy.

# I Keep On Bleeding

I keep on bleeding.

My hematologist says
I don't have VonWillebrand's,
I have senile purpura.
My dermatologist says
These days we just call it
Purpura. My brother seems
To have a touch of Azeheimers.
I seem to have senile dimmentia,
Like FDR. Do we just call it
Dimentia these days?
A friend has early onset
Parkinson's. What will late
Onset look like? Ah, the
Vissitudes of senile living.

# Rabbits Big as a House

We had an old yellow dog
Who was twitching in his sleep.
William had little speech then
After his stroke, but he looked
Down and said, "rabbits, big as
A house." I knew William was
Still in there, his humor in tact.
A moment of hope in a dark time.

# If Need Be

If need be, my therapist's
Wife will wipe his ass.
This is not gross,
This is love.

He calls his children
Kiddos as though they
were born in the 40s.

He is an Italian wolf
With dimples. I wish
I were his age. I wish
I were his wife.

# Commercial

In the commercial, a new mom
Let's the black lab puppy sleep
On her belly. A man, with a
beautiful voice sings, "I will love
You forever."
                We see mother playing
With her new daughter at the beach.
The black dog, Elsie, champion
At frisbee, despite a snout which
Grown a bit gray.

They are on their way home,
Perhaps to hospice care.

The puppy remembers the baby
Thrashing about in the womb. He
Will love them both forever; he runs
With joy like the little girl
Anxious to greet life inside
Her belly, now become a private
Respite after the final birth.

"I will love you forever," the man
Sings again. I will buy whatever he
Is selling, like Elsie. forever.

# Going to Ghana

Daddy has a horse tail
Fom when he played rugby.
He needs a raminectomy.
He can't pee or poo.

The pictures of Ghana
On TV show jungles where
You can hide, pretty
beaches where you can
Swim. Daddy please, oh
Please can we go to Ghana.

# My Therapist

My therapist has a black beard
Since I saw him last. He looks
Like an Italian wolf with dimples.
I told him at one point I'd give
Him a hundred dollards if he
Would drop his pants. He points
To his marriage ring. He is quite
Serious. But occasionally, he
Bends over in front of me.
Freudian? Jungian? Something
Is at work in his imagination.

# Parallel

2016
72" x 72"
Acrylic Enamel and mixed media on canvas

# Drink Coke

The man in the moon
Drinks Coke a Cola.
He likes it so much
He's going to turn the
Moon into a giant ad,
Visible from the earth:
DRINK COKE.

# Betty is Spaying

When my brother-in-law's
Rottweiler comes into heat
Betty is spayed and chipped
And comes home with that
Funny collar that keeps her
From chewing at the stitches.
No puppies for you Betty,
Now you can focus
On John and Juddi

## Sydney at Rest

She sleeps at my feet
Like a medieval dog
Asleep in stone at the
Feet of a knight sleeping
In stone in the curuches
Of Portugal, her long legs
Folded in elegant rest
After the hunt is done.

In the spring, in green grass
She turns lavender. Then
She is a dog fit for a saint.
She glows, and is ready
For the chase. Evil is no
Match for her. But now
She husband's her energy
Until she is called to duty.

# You Snooze, You Lose

You Snooze, You Lose

I quartered seven apples,
Devained them of stems
And seeds, all 28 pieces
Has a special New Year's
Treat for the deer. I took
Them surreptitiously to
The middle of the field
When, swoosh, a flock of
Seigle landed to gobble
Them up like Cape Cod
Chips at the beach,
Every single piece.

You snooze you lose
My dears.

# Viking

He's a big guy. I mean
Really big. He can lift my
Toilet with his bare hands
When it comes time to
Replace my bathroom floor.

"Where's the SUPER,"
The other tenants want to know
When they see my toilet in the
Hall. They want to track him
Down to fix a light switch or
Replace a bulb.
                    "Beats me,"
I tell them. "Go knock on his door."

# The Head Honcho

The head honcho
Here at Senile housing
Says a snow storm
Is coming. She puts up
Lists at the elevator and
In the community room
Where are you have to move
Your car to clear space
For the snow plows.

She ends her memo with
Stay indoors at all costs.

How to get my walker through
A foot of snow to move my car
Is the question. I'm going back
To bed. Snow plough will
Just have to do the best he can.

# Evicted

The small starlings of winter took up residence
In the rhododendron outside my window.
I would watch them, drole d'equip like a herd of
Meerkats keeping an eye out in the neighborhood for danger.
They would pop up like Jack in the box, black, gray and brown, their
Eyes like small rapt beads taking it all in.

Then the maintenance man came
With his wind blower and flushed them into a legend.
These are the birds of the air that Jesus spoke of.
They will find another home.
But what am I to do, like them, evicted, unable to fly.

# Trump's Election

"He cannot shake his unpopular conviction
That his nation has bitterly misspoken itself."

From "Nixon's the One" by William Meredith

The pundits say "Fear and anger"
Drove the nation to elect Trump.
At any rate, they have their darling and
I am almost ashamed to be a citizen.
Fasten your seatbelts for four more years.

Kamala instructs us to be kind now,
Forgiveness and letting go of the grudge.
We survived Regan and he wound up
Bringing down the wall. Who knows how
It will turn out. One too many hamburgers,
And we will be stuck with Vance. Nothing
Lasts forever. I'm glad I'm not a cat lady
Or even trans. Tough times are in store
For women, men too. We can not let
Fear and anger be our guiding light.

# Condensation

The cherry strips I use to keep
My breathing fresh, have gone orange.
Now when I speak, orange blossoms
Fill the air. Four letter words like
F, S, and C choke me up.
I cannot curse properly.
My CPAP machine is like
Breathing ambrosia.
Apple peach and almond
Transport me to springtime
In southern France. Breathing
Now is better than dreaming.
If this mysterious conversion
Could only change my heartbeat
Or how my stomach works,
My spirit would not be far behind,
A fountainhead of love and compassion
Like melting ice, or water
Evaporating into cloud.

# Guardian

2016
72" x 72"
Acrylic Enamel and mixed media on canvas

# About the Author
# Richar Harteis

Poet and novelist RICHARD HARTEIS is the President of the William Meredith Foundation and directs Poets Choice Publishing House. He served for two years as a Peace Corps volunteer in Tunisia, worked as a physician assistant in North Africa and Asia and spent a Fulbright year as writer-in-residence at the American University in Bulgaria. At the end of that year, he was accorded Bulgarian citizenship by decree of the President and Parliament in 1996.

He has written 14 books of prose and poetry and edited and introduced 12 books with publishers here and abroad. In 2019, he received a fifth award for his screenplay, COMES LOVE which has been scheduled for production by the Hollywood Dreams Film Festival directors.

His work has received honors and awards including fellowships from the National Endowment for the Arts, the D.C. Commission on the Arts, the Ford Foundation, Creighton University and the Catholic University of America. After the death of his partner of 36 years, the poet William Meredith, their home, "Riverrun," was added to the Connecticut Registry of Historic Places in 2007. He lives in Connecticut with his Australian cattle dog, Sydney.

# Sanket Patel Biography
# Graphic Designer

Sanket Patel is an experienced 33-year-old graphic designer, illustrator, and web designer from Connecticut. He was born in India and moved to the states at age five. He developed a strong appreciation for the cultures of both India and the United States. His style as an artist incorporates his Indian roots and expresses this culture in a modern and innovative way. He has several years of experience, working in a multitude of design roles and settings. Sanket has become a very sought-after designer, and is able to bring a creative, and professional approach to any project.

# Anne Marchand Biography
## Artist

Anne Marchand was born in New Orleans. She majored in art at Auburn University, graduating with a BA, and then earned an MFA from the University of Georgia. Her early artistic focus was the figure, and she was especially drawn to the work of Francis Bacon for his expressive paintings of the human body. Marchand's other early influences include 20th century modernist painters, the Abstract Expressionists, and the work of Carl Jung, with his reflections on dream imagery and psychological states. She credits her upbringing in New Orleans for her sensitivity to, "a sense of awe at the power and majesty of nature."

In 2005, Marchand's Ellipsis paintings, with their arcing lines and vivid color, expressed her desire to create "cosmoscapes", inspired by deep space. Mystical themes came to the fore in the paintings, stimulated by readings by Garcia Lorca, Kandinsky, and Rumi. Travel to India brought a range of new color palettes and fabrics that she incorporated into her work.

Beginning in 2010, Marchand began experimenting in paintings with acrylic mediums and interference and pearlescent pigments. With these materials, qualities of radiance and light became active metaphors reflecting an inner state of being. Images of planets from the Hubble telescope inspired the painter to introduce circular imagery into her work. The nebulas and galaxies suggested biological structures, and Marchand realized the connection between space and the body as manifestations.

# Rick Williams Biography
# Back Cover Painter

Rick Williams was on active duty in the army from July 1969 to February 1971, including 13 months at the *3rd Surgical Army Hospital (MASH)* in *Binh Thuy, Vietnam*, serving as a medical corpsman in the intensive care unit; as a physician assistant (PA) employed by the *Veterans Medical Center* in *New Orleans* under the psychiatry service; and as a lawyer and judge with the *Board of Veterans Appeals* in *Washington, D.C.* In the latter position, he authored over a thousand appellate decisions.

Williams also studied art at the *Corcoran School of Art* (nights) in *Washington, D.C.* Seven of his paintings are part of the permanent collection of the National *Veterans Art Museum* (formerly *National Vietnam Art Museum*) in *Chicago, Illinois*. His portraits of veterans wounded or killed in action are part of the permanent collections of the *VA Regional Offices* in *New York City* and *Buffalo, New York*. Rick's art exhibits *"Infinitely Complex"*, which had mental illness as theme; and *"Ravages of Addiction"* held at *Casa de Arte* in *Buffalo, New York* in 2012 and 2016, were well reviewed by art critics from *Artvoice, The Public*, and the *Buffalo News*.

Williams completed the *University of Iowa's Summer Creative Writers' Workshop* in May-June 2019.

He resides in *Bethesda, Maryland*, and *Cuernavaca, Morelos, Mexico*.

# Richard Harteis

Portrait by Rick Williams
Private Collection

www.ingramcontent.com/pod-product-compliance
Lightning Source LLC
Chambersburg PA
CBHW040209100526
44585CB00002BA/18